Skating SUPERSTARS

SCHOLASTIC INC.

New York Toronto London Auckland Sydney Mexico City New Delhi Hong Kong

UNAUTHORIZED: This book is not sponsored by or
affiliated with the stars or anyone involved with them.

Produced by Shoreline Publishing Group LLC
Cover Design: Bill Madrid
Text by James Buckley, Jr.

Cover photos: Front: AP/Wide World; Back: Getty Images: Timothy A. Clary/AFP (bottom);
Harry How (top); Chung Sung-Jun (left).
Interior: AP/Wide World: 4; all others by Getty Images; photographers listed here: AFP: 18;
Timothy A. Clary/AFP: 30; Doug Pensinger: 28; Kevork Djansezian: 29; Harry How: 10, 14,
16, 17, 23, 25, 26; Junko Kimura: 13; Kiyoshi Ota: 20; Mark Ralston: 5, 9, 11, 12, 22, 24.

ISBN: 978-0-545-20730-0

10 9 8 7 6 5 4 3 2 1   09 10 11 12 13
Printed in the USA   23
First printing, December 2009

CONTENTS

INTRODUCTION

The arena lights go out, except for those shining on the ice. The crowd stills, and silence fills the slightly chilly air. Then the music starts . . . and the magic begins! Figure skaters glide almost effortlessly across the ice. Their costumes shimmer in the lights—their talent is just as sparkling. As they leap, the crowd holds its breath. As they land safely, applause fills the air.

★ Jessica Dubé and Bryce Davison of Canada show how pairs skaters must glide in perfect harmony. ★

The music rises and falls, and then the show is over. . . . Breathless, the skaters bow to the cheers of an adoring crowd.

Figure skaters combine art, grace, and beauty with amazing physical ability. Few other sports demand such a combination of style and sweat. The skaters, timing their moves to the music, stride, leap, spin, and almost seem to fly.

They do it all on a knife edge between success and disaster. The blade of a figure skate is less than one eighth of an inch wide. It's hard to imagine doing such tricks in sneakers, let alone ice skates. One slip or one false move can end in catastrophe.

Skaters compete in several major events. Two of the biggest are the annual World Championships and the United States Championships. But the one they are all aiming for comes just every four years.

The Winter Olympics is the prime showcase for figure skaters. The sport is the most-watched event of the Games around the world, with tens of millions of people tuning in to watch the ladies' individual finals alone. At the Winter Olympics in Vancouver,

Figure Skating

Here are the four major types of figure skating competitions:

- ⭐ Ladies' Individual
- ⭐ Men's Individual
- ⭐ Pairs (one male and one female skater)
- ⭐ Ice Dance* (one male and one female skater)

* In ice dance, the moves are more dancelike than the acrobatic pairs event.

★ American Sasha Cohen finished second at the 2006 Olympics. ★

Canada, in February 2010, which stars will make it to the winners' podium?

Let's meet some of these amazing athletes and find out how they are skating their way to the top.

Yu-Na KIM

Yu-Na Kim had been working her way up the ladder steadily for several years, and in 2009, she reached the top of the figure skating world. With a nearly flawless routine, she won the World Championships gold medal in Los Angeles, thanks to her graceful, flowing style combined with perfect jumps and landings.

Yu-Na was a five-time National Champion in her native South Korea. In fact, she was only 12 when she won that title for the first time!

In 2006, she became the first Korean skater to win a world title when she became the World Junior Champion. That year, she moved to Canada to train with former Canadian superstar Brian Orser.

★ Yu-Na shows off a sit spin, in which a skater spins very quickly while in a sitting position. The move combines speed with great body control and style. ★

Brian helped Yu-Na add some difficult jumps to her routines. They developed a type of camel spin that has been named after her, the Yu-Na spin.

The long hours they worked together in the rink paid off. In 2007 and 2008, Yu-Na was the bronze medalist (third place) in the World Championships.

Since 2006, figure skating has had a points-based judging system that rewards success and style. At the World Championships in 2009, Yu-Na set a new record with a short program (first round) score of

★ In the Yu-Na spin, the skater extends one leg to the rear and then spins around and around on her other leg. It demands great balance and precision. ★

★ Yu-Na's world title made her a hero back home in Korea. ★

76.12, and she performed beautifully in the final free skate. Her final total of 207.71 points made her the first to top 200 points under the new system. Yu-Na proudly brought her championship medal back to Korea. Will she be carrying more medals back home from the Winter Olympics in 2010?

Japanese STARS

A pair of Japanese female skaters are among the world's best. They'll probably be among the challengers for Olympic gold.

Mao Asada was the 2008 World Champion after winning three Japanese national titles. She is a powerful skater who excels in jumps while also showing off a graceful style. In 2006, she became the first female to land two triple Axels. (The triple Axel is a jump during which

⭐ Mao shows her flexibility while performing this move, in which she grabs her skate over her head while spinning on the other skate. ⭐

★ Like Mao, Miki went from being the champion of Japan to being champion of the world. ★

the skater spins three and a half times before landing!)

In 2008, Mao won the World Championship even though she fell once at the start of her free skate. She was happy to share her joy with her dog, Aero. Mao and Aero have been in commercials for chocolate on Japanese TV!

Miki Ando is a rising star from the Land of the Rising Sun. A two-time Japanese champion, she is also, like Mao, a former World Champion (2007). When she was only 15, she became the first female to hit a quadruple jump! In 2009, she was third overall at the World Championships.

★ Joannie will have the hometown crowd on her side at the 2010 Olympics in Canada. They've watched her win five Canadian championships. ★

Joannie ROCHETTE

It's not surprising that a northern land like Canada has produced a world-class skating star. Joannie Rochette is the latest in a long line of Canadian ice queens and kings.

Joannie started skating when she was six years old. She was the first skater to win Canada's national titles at every level. She had one of her best events yet at the 2009 World Championships, finishing second to Yu-Na Kim. Joannie's glamorous style and solid jumps earned raves from the judges and long applause from the fans.

Her experience during the 2006 Winter Olympics, where she finished fifth, will be valuable as she continues to go for the gold in 2010!

Rachael FLATT

Let's meet America's top skaters! One of the best is Rachael Flatt. She is only 17 years old . . . but she's already the 2008 World Junior Champion! Competing against more experienced skaters, she's done nearly as well, twice finishing second at the U.S. National Championships.

In 2009, she finished fifth at the World Championships, the highest finish by any American skater that year. She did six triple jumps in her free skate, marking her as a skater to watch in the future. Also in 2009, she

★ Rachael has her skates packed for a trip to Vancouver . . . but first she has to earn a place on the final American Olympic team, which will be picked in early 2010. ★

helped the United States win its first World Team Trophy. In that event, skaters from several countries competed. Their points were added up, and the U.S. team had the highest score!

Now that she has graduated from high school in Colorado (where she had a 4.0 GPA), Rachael has her sights set on a spot in Olympic skating history.

★ "Everything I do counts toward that ultimate goal of competing [in the Olympics]," Rachael wrote on her Web site in 2009. ★

★ When she's not skating or doing one of her many other activities, Alissa goes to college in Ohio, where she studies international relations. ★

Alissa CZISNY

It's hard to imagine where Alissa Czisny (SIZ-nee) finds the time to skate. The 2009 U.S. Champion also loves to go rock climbing and biking, learn languages, practice ballet, and act!

On the ice, she made her big move by winning the 2009 U.S. title. She might not jump as high or as often as some other skaters, but few have as much elegance and grace as Alissa. She always skates with a smile on her face. All that ballet must be paying off!

At the World Championships in 2009, she was disappointed with her eleventh-place finish. But that will make her that much more determined in the battle for a spot on the Olympic team.

For his big moment in the spotlight at the World Championships, Evan wore a skating costume that looked like a tuxedo!

Evan LYSACEK

As he finished his final spin at the 2009 World Championships, Evan Lysacek (LIES-uh-chek) knew his dream was coming true. His long road was reaching its highest point. Thousands of hours of effort were paying off.

Evan put on a nearly perfect free skate. He showed off his great athletic ability with several triple jumps. The fans in Los Angeles loved it!

After the final skaters had their shot to top his routine, it was official: Evan was the World Champion! He was the first American male skater to win that title since Todd Eldredge in 1996.

What's even more amazing is that Evan did all this with a broken bone in his foot. He ignored the pain and triumphed!

★ Evan's style combines great jumping ability with super spins. ★

Evan got his start as a skater while he was living in Chicago. By the time he was 13, he was the National Novice Champion. He became the National Junior Champion the next year in 2000. By 2004, he finished third in the World Junior Championships, and he was fourth at the 2006 Winter Olympics.

Along with his talent, Evan stands out among skaters for another reason. Most skaters are not very tall. However, Evan grew to be six feet two inches.

His height might have been a disadvantage, but he turned it into one of his best tools. He worked with choreographer Lori Nichol, who encouraged Evan to try moves that would set him apart from other skaters. (A choreographer is a person who helps plan dance or skating routines.) Evan has been the highest American finisher in the world each year since 2005.

He capped that off with his 2009 world title. While he prepares to go for the gold in Vancouver, Evan also spends time helping others. He is active in the Make-a-Wish Foundation and Ronald McDonald House. All the kids he helps are hoping Evan sees his own dreams come true!

★ Evan hopes to be holding an American flag . . . and a gold medal . . . at the end of the 2010 Winter Olympics. ★

Top Male SKATERS

★ Can Patrick Chan thrill his hometown fans in Canada by winning Olympic gold? ★

Evan Lysacek will be up against a hometown favorite in Vancouver. Patrick Chan is from Ottawa, Ontario, and will have the maple leaf flags flying in Canada. He's the two-time Canadian Champion and finished second to Evan at the 2009 Worlds. He's a great athlete and takes part in tennis, skiing, and tae kwon do.

If not for a slight stumble in the free skate at the 2009 World Championships, Brian Joubert might have stolen the title from Evan Lysacek. The six-time French Champion knows what it takes. In 2007, he was the World Champion himself. In 2004, he was the first Frenchman in 40 years to win the European championship.

"I came here to win the gold medal," Brian said after the 2009 event. "I won the bronze medal. I am a little bit disappointed, but I have to use this World Championship to be better for the next season."

★ Brian overcame the loss of a kidney when he was a baby to become a six-time French skating champion. ★

★ German pairs skaters Robin Szolkowy (top) and Aliona Savchenko have been skating together since 2003. ★

Pairs SKATERS

Skating is hard enough just by yourself. The athletes who take part in pairs skating skate together as smoothly and beautifully as one. Pairs skaters often use "throws," in which the male skater tosses the female skater in the air. She does amazing gymnastics in midair and then lands (they hope!) cleanly and gracefully.

Skaters must skate side by side or opposite each other. They also team up to do amazing spins. One kind of spin is called the "death spiral." The female skater is pulled around and around with her head just inches from the ice!

In 2009, pairs skaters from Germany, Aliona Savchenko and Robin Szolkowy, won their second straight World Championships.

A pair of Russian skaters will be among the challengers for the gold. Actually, only half of this team is from Russia, though they represent that country. Yuko Kawaguchi grew up in Japan. She teamed up with Alexander Smirnov in 2006, and they have quickly become among the world's best. They had high finishes at the 2008 and 2009 European Championships. At the 2009 World Championships, they placed third. Will they land on the Olympic medal podium next? The top U.S. pairs skaters are Keauna McLaughlin and Rockne Brubaker.

★ Alexander Smirnov (bottom) tosses his partner, Yuko Kawaguchi. Don't worry . . . he's going to catch her! ★

★ Colorful, flashy, and stylish, the U.S. pair of Keauna McLaughlin and Rockne Brubaker are the best American team. ★

Though they have only been together since 2006, they have already won two U.S. Championships and a World Junior Championships. The pair had a tough time at the 2009 Worlds, finishing eleventh after making mistakes. However, they hope to bounce back and earn a place in Vancouver in 2010.

Ice DANCE

Like pairs skating, ice dance is two skaters working together as a team. In ice dance, however, the skaters must be touching nearly all the time and the moves are more dancelike than gymnastic. Grace and style count more than throws, lifts, and jumps.

The top American hope for ice dance gold is the team of Tanith Belbin and Ben Agosto. They have won five U.S. Championships. Both have been skating since not long after they learned to walk! They teamed up in 1998 and have a shelf full of medals and trophies. In 2009, they added a World Championships silver medal. They earned silver at the 2006 Olympics. Can they bring home gold in 2010?

Winning gold at the 2009 World Championships was the Russian pair of Oksana Domnina and Maxim Shabalin. Though they train alongside the American stars, once the event begins, they battle to win!

★ Ice dancers often skate to different types of music. Tanith Belbin and Ben Agosto choose costumes to match the tune. ★

GLOSSARY

Axel a type of jump in which a skater takes off on one foot and lands on the other after completing one and a half rotations.

edge the outside of each skate blade. Skaters use the outside or inside edges of their skates to make turns and jumps.

flip a kind of jump in which the skater uses the toe of one skate to help them leap off the ice.

lift used in pairs, it's when the male skater holds the female above his head.

Lutz a kind of jump made while going backward.

Salchow a kind of jump taken from the inside edge of one foot and landed on the outside edge of the opposite foot.

sit spin a spin done on one skate while nearly sitting on the ice, with the other foot held out in front of the body.

toe loop a type of jump in which the skater takes off and lands on the same edge of the skate.

throw a move in pairs skating in which the male tosses the female into the air, where she does several spins before landing.

Note: The Axel, Lutz, and Salchow are all named for the male skaters who invented the jumps.